Inspired by James and Oli

Text and Illustrations Copyright © Christopher Paul 2024

Illustrations by Kris Lillyman 2024

Moral rights asserted

The right of Christopher Paul and Kris Lillyman to be identified as the Author and Illustrator of this work has been asserted by them in accordance with the Copyright, Design and Patents Act 1988.

All rights reserved. No part of this publication may be reproduced, stored in a retrieval system, or transmitted, in any form, or by any means (electronic, mechanical, photocopying, recording or otherwise) without the prior written permission of the publisher.

Christopher Paul

Jacob's Cats

Illustrated by Kris Lillyman

All of them, the pets and the strays, would spend a great deal of time on the allotments doing what cats do. And this was the problem. Jacob loved his allotment. But often when Jacob went weeding or digging he would get cat poo on his spade or on his fork, or even on his hands. And it drove him bonkers.

Jacob spoke to the men in the pub about it. "What you need," said one of the men, "is a water pistol. Cats hate water. You squirt those cats a couple of times, they'll soon get the message." So Jacob bought a water pistol.

Jacob filled the water pistol from his water butt and sat down in his shed, keeping watch through the open door. He smiled to himself, poured a cup of tea from his flask and waited. And waited...

Jacob was awoken by the sound of the shed door banging shut in a sudden breeze.
Sitting up quickly, he spilled his tea onto his lap.
Jumping up angrily, he hit his head on the low shed roof.

Swearing loudly, he stumbled through the door, tripped over his spade and landed flat on his face a few inches away from a newly-laid poo.

The next day, Jacob took Daggers to the allotment. He put a piece of rope through the dog's collar, tied it to the shed door and got on with his digging. When the first cat came near, Daggers barked loudly and the cat ran away. Jacob smiled and went into his shed to have a nice cup of tea.

But when he came out, there, next to Daggers, was a great big poo. A dog poo. Jacob smacked his forehead.

The men in the pub laughed when Jacob told them about Daggers. "What you need to do," they said, "is to stop worrying about cats. Cheer up, Jacob."

But Jacob didn't cheer up. On his way home, he went past the allotments and peered through the railings. It was getting dark but he could hear his shed door banging in the wind. He would have to sort that out.

Then it all went horribly wrong. As Jacob reached his shed he tripped on the rope which was still tied to the door. He fell backwards and bumped his head on the water butt. He couldn't get up. He couldn't move. Jacob lay there, eyes closed, with the cold wind snatching away the steam from his breath.

That night a sharp frost came to the gardens and the allotments, and the pet cats stayed indoors, sitting in front of fires or curling up in their baskets. Outside the strays shivered and howled as they searched desperately for somewhere warm to sleep.

But Jacob didn't want to rest. He had work to do. He went straight to the allotment and there he spent the day, not digging, not weeding, but instead making a cat flap in his shed door.

Printed in Great Britain
by Amazon